I wonder...
HOW DO
SUBMARINES DIVE?

Written by Andrew Langley
Illustrated by Stuart Trotter

Why do houses creak at night?

A house is made of many kinds of materials. It may be built of stone, brick, or wood. There is glass in the windows and there may be concrete in the floors.

During the day, the sun warms up the house. The bricks, wood, and other materials get hotter. The heat makes them swell slightly, or expand.

At night, it is colder. The bricks and wood cool down again. They get smaller, or contract.

As they contract, the materials in the house rub against each other. This can cause little creaks and groans.

Why do radiators gurgle?

Many houses are kept warm by radiators. The radiators are full of water that is heated by a boiler.

The hot water from the boiler is pumped along pipes through each of the radiators. Then the water cools, and it is pumped back to the boiler to be heated again.

BLOOP!

Sometimes, bubbles of air become trapped inside the pipes and radiators. The bubbles gurgle as they move through the pipes.

How can water burst a pipe?

When water freezes, it takes up more space, or expands. Even if the ice is trapped in a pipe, it will still expand. The ice pushes outward and bursts the pipe. When the ice melts again, water will leak out of the burst.

How does water come out of a faucet?

When rain falls, it runs into streams and rivers. In some places, the water is collected in huge lakes, called reservoirs.

Next, the water must be cleaned. It is pumped to special water treatment plants, where it is filtered and chemicals are added to make it safe.

The clean water is pumped through underground pipes to our homes.

In the house, the water may be stored in a big tank. When we turn on a faucet, the water flows from the tank and into the sink.

Where does the bath water go?

When we have used our clean water, we let it drain away. It flows out of the house through waste pipes.

The waste water then flows into a much bigger pipe called a sewer. There, it joins the waste water from many other houses.

Waste water is very dirty. The sewer carries it to a sewage plant, where the germs and heavy dirt are removed. Then it can be pumped away to rivers or the sea.

Where does dust come from?

Dust is everywhere, even though we can't always see it. It floats in the air and settles on everything.

Outdoors, dust is mostly made of specks of rock and soot. In summer, dust also contains pollen grains from grass and other plants.

Some outdoor dust gets into the house. It blows in through windows and doors. Some gets carried in on our shoes and clothes.

Outdoor dust mixes with dust already indoors. A lot of indoor dust is made of human skin. Very tiny flakes drop from our skin all the time.

How do refrigerators stay cold?

At the back of a refrigerator are thin tubes. These tubes contain a special liquid that will easily turn into a gas, or vapor. All it needs is a little heat.

The liquid is pumped along the tubes into the refrigerator. It absorbs any heat that may be inside the refrigerator, and then turns into a gas.

The gas is pumped back through the tubes on the outside of the refrigerator, taking the heat with it. The gas cools down and turns back into a liquid. This makes the inside of the refrigerator colder.

How does a telephone work?

When we speak, the noise makes the air shake, or vibrate. This creates waves of sound, which we can't see.

Inside a telephone mouthpiece is a thin sheet of metal called a diaphragm. When we speak into the mouthpiece, we make the metal vibrate.

The shaking of the metal sheet is turned into an electrical message. This travels along the telephone wire to the person listening.

Inside the earpiece of the other telephone is another metal diaphragm in the earpiece. The message makes the sheet vibrate and give an exact copy of the words that we spoke.

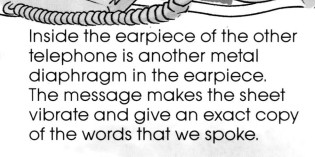

Why do windows steam up?

The air contains thousands and thousands of very tiny water droplets called vapor. Usually, we can't see it.

Sometimes, warm vapor touches a cold surface, such as a window. The vapor quickly cools down and turns into liquid water on the glass. Now we can see it — the window has steamed up.

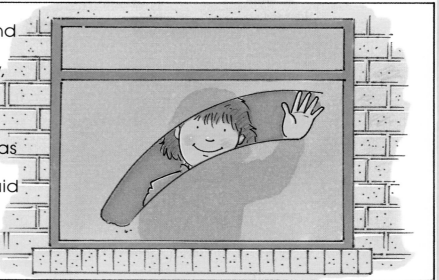

Why do some balloons float?

If we blow up a balloon with our own breath, it won't float in the air. The reason is our breath is heavier than the air.

If a balloon is filled with a special gas called helium, it will float. Why? Because helium is much lighter than the air.

How does a radio work?

A radio can send sounds all over the world. The sounds, such as speech or music, are first turned into electrical signals. These invisible signals are called radio waves.

The radio waves travel through the air. When the waves reach our radio sets, they are turned back into sounds.

Where does a TV picture come from?

Pictures can travel on radio waves too. A TV camera scans the picture in front of it line by line. Each line is turned into electrical signals.

The radio waves carry the signals to our TV sets. Line by line, the TV set turns the signals back into a picture.

What makes soda pop fizzy?

Soda pop isn't always fizzy. At first it is an unfizzy liquid. Then a gas called carbon dioxide is bubbled through it.

Most of the carbon dioxide dissolves into the liquid. The drink is then poured into a bottle and sealed up tight.

As long as the drink stays sealed up, the gas will remain dissolved. It can't escape, because there is no room in the bottle or can.

As soon as the bottle is opened, the gas will start to escape. It turns into bubbles, shoots to the top of the liquid, and goes into the air.

How does a microwave oven work?

Inside a microwave oven is an electronic tube. This sends out special radio waves. The waves go into the food in the oven.

All food has some water or fat in it. Water and fat are made up of tiny particles called molecules.

The radio waves make the water and fat molecules shake. They shake so much that they get hot. The food heats up and cooks very quickly.

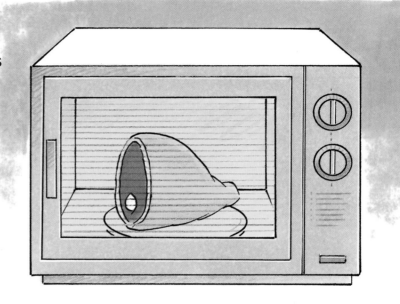

Why do plates stay cold in a microwave oven?

Plates are made of china or glass. They have no fat or water molecules in them. The radio waves pass through plates without heating them up.

Why does my hair crackle sometimes?

Everything around us contains tiny particles called electrons. When electrons move from one thing to another, they produce energy. We call this electricity.

Sometimes electrons collect in one place. If you comb your hair, electrons from your hair may stick to the comb.

Now the comb has lots of electrons, but your hair has few. If you go on combing, the electrons will jump back onto your hair.

As they jump, the electrons crackle. This is called static electricity.

What makes a light bulb glow?

Inside a light bulb is a tiny coil of thin wire. When the light is switched on, electricity flows through the wire.

The wire becomes very hot and glows white. The glass around the bulb spreads the glow and gives out a strong, steady light.

How does a vacuum cleaner work?

Inside a vacuum cleaner is an electric motor with a fan. The fan spins very quickly, pushing air out of the cleaner through a hole.

More air rushes in through another hole to fill the space that is left. As the air enters, it sucks up dirt. The dirt is trapped in a bag inside the vacuum cleaner.

How does an airplane lift off the ground?

It is the special shape of the airplane's wings that help lift it off the ground. But to climb into the air, an airplane must travel forward very fast.

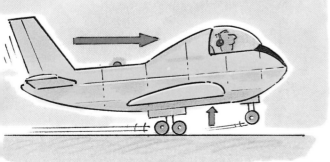

As the plane moves forward, air flows over and under the wings. Because the top surface is curved, it is longer than the bottom. The air has farther to go.

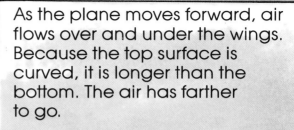
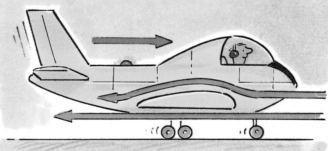

The air traveling over the wings flows faster than the air under the wings. The slow-moving air underneath pushes the wings upward.

The airplane's strong engines push it faster and faster through the air. The pilot raises the nose of the airplane, and it rises into the sky.

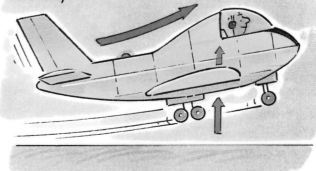

What is glass made of?

Glass is mostly made of sand. This is mixed with soda (sodium oxide), lime, and pieces of old glass. The mixture is heated in a giant furnace.

The mixture melts and turns into a liquid. Then it can be poured into a mold, where it cools and turns into solid glass.

A blob of molten glass can also be put on the end of a long hollow tube and blown into shape like a bubble.

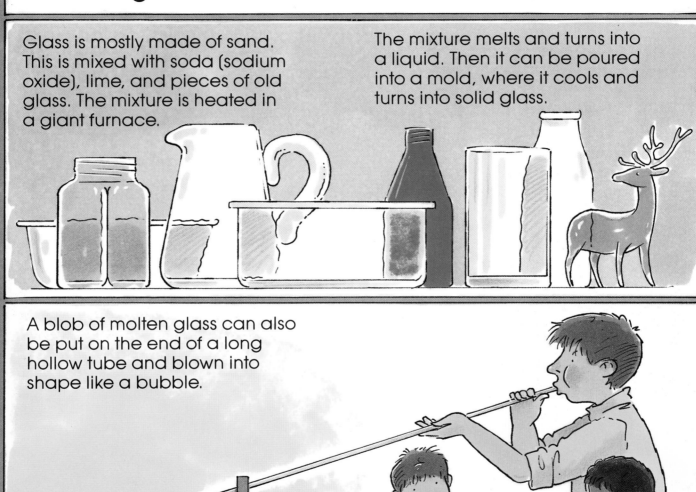

How does a magnifying glass work?

A magnifying glass has two curved sides. The curves make light bend and spread out.

When we look at something through a magnifying glass, it seems bigger. Why? Because the light bouncing off the object has been spread out by the glass.

Why can I see myself in a mirror?

A mirror has two parts. The front is a sheet of plain glass. At the back is a thin sheet of shiny metal.

Light bouncing off you travels to the mirror. Then the light travels through the glass, bounces off the shiny metal, and comes back to you. You can see your own light.

Why does a boat stay afloat?

Gravity is a force which pulls things down toward the earth. When you throw a ball into the air, gravity pulls it down again.

When a boat is in the water, part of it is under the surface. Gravity has pulled it down toward the earth.

But the boat doesn't sink. This is because the water is pushing upward at the same time.

The boat has taken up some room in the water. Now the water is pushing to fill up that room again. As it pushes, it forces the boat upward. The boat stays afloat.

How does a submarine dive?

Air is lighter than water. A boat is full of air, so it floats. If it were filled with water, it would sink.

A submarine is a boat that can float or sink. It has special air tanks on its sides. These keep it afloat.

When water is let into the tanks, the air goes out. The submarine is now heavier than water, and dives down into the sea.

Then air is pumped back into the tanks. It pushes out the water. Now the submarine is lighter than water again, and floats to the surface.

GLOSSARY

A list and explanation of some of the terms used in this book.

Carbon dioxide
— a tasteless, colorless gas that can be used to make still drinks fizzy.

Contract
— to shrink or become shorter. Many materials contract when they become cold.

Diaphragm
— a thin dividing layer of material.

Electricity
— a type of energy that is used to produce light, heat and power for machines.

Electron
— a tiny particle that carries the smallest possible amount of electricity.

Expand
— to become larger. Many materials expand when they become warm.

Gravity
— the force that pulls things toward the ground.

Microwave
— a type of radio wave with a very short wavelength.

Molecule
— the smallest particle into which a substance can be divided and keep its chemical properties.

Static electricity
— electricity that does not flow in a curre but stays in one place.

Vapor
— a liquid that has been warmed and h turned into an invisible gas.